MW01503014

OPTIONS
VS
FOREX & FUTURES

A PRAGMATIC GUIDE FOR BEGINNER TRADERS.
LEARN HOW TO PRACTICE BY USING
DEMOS AND SIMULATORS

John B. Stevenson

Options Vs. Forex & Futures

Table of Contents

Introduction

O ne significant term associated with options is derivatives. If you have been in the world of stocks for some time, then you will be well aware of this condition and what it brings to the table. At the core of it, derivatives are underlying goods or products that help people earn their incentives. For example, if an apple pie is delicious, then the reason for it will be fresh apples, fresh ingredients, and the chef's skills. Similarly, for a financial instrument to do well, many derivatives should work in its favor and should be obtained at a reasonable price.

This trading depends heavily on the prices of the products or other such conditions. Options trading is nothing but a contract between two or more parties, usually the buyer and the seller.

It is all about providing an option to the buyer that a particular asset can be valuable in the future. The seller of the commodity will get a fee or a small amount of money as a reservation of the option. The seller then guarantees that he will keep the option and sell it in full once the buyer pays the total amount.

Options happen to be an excellent strategy for those looking to expand their portfolio in the stock world. There are many types of options to choose from, and the buyer can settle for one that is going to make him the most profit. It is exceptionally easy for those who have practiced hedging and are well versed in how the stock market operates.

CHAPTER 1:

What are Futures?

The futures market today is a large, mostly electronic set of exchanges where traders can go to buy or sell contracts.

Popular products include futures on stock indexes, energy, currencies, bonds, metals, and agricultural commodities.

Players in the futures market include hedgers, who are the people looking to manage risk for existing assets such as inventories of crude oil, silos full of soybeans, or portfolios of stocks.

Speculators, on the other hand, attempt to generate profits from the price moves of the futures contract and do not intend to take delivery of (or to deliver, in the case of a short trade) the physical commodity.

Most brokers won't let you take delivery anyway.

They will close out your trade before the expiration of the contract, which is good, except they won't care if you are in a winning or losing position.

They will liquidate your position rather than let 1,000 barrels of crude oil end up on your doorstep.

o **How the Futures Market Works**

Although there are still a handful of trading pits, the days of traders screaming out orders and throwing up hand signals are mostly a thing of the past. Instead, the bulk of futures transactions are done electronically. Buying and selling happen in milliseconds, with a trader taking the short side of every long position and vice versa.

Each contract is standardized, which means that the specific terms (expirations, quantities, quality standards, and symbols) are clearly spelled out in the contract. Standardizing makes it easier for market participants to understand the nuances of each specific contract.

All futures are contracts, agreements to buy or sell an underlying asset at a set price and at a specific time. An underlying asset can be crude oil futures, gold, a stock market index, or several other financial instruments. Futures contracts trade up and down in the market, just like stocks

Futures contracts are not typically held through the expiration, however, and a trader can close or cover a long contract at any time by selling the same contract. Conversely, futures contracts can be sold when the price is expected to fall. A short futures position is covered with a purchase or buys order, which is sometimes called an offsetting purchase.

Prices for futures are often different from the price of the underlying asset. On the one hand, there is the cash price, or spot price, which is the actual price of the commodity or financial instrument and the price of the physical commodity or investment today. On the other hand, there is the futures price, which reflects expectations about the future and consideration of other costs like storage, transportation, and interest.

Futures contracts are bought and sold using margin. That is, the trader must provide a deposit and maintain a certain level of funds for each long or short futures position. The deposit is called the initial margin and is typically 5% to 15% of the value of the contract size. After that, the account must meet the maintenance margin or face a margin call.

- Initial Margin: The initial deposit made when buying or selling a futures contract; ranges between 5% and 15% of the value of the futures contract size.

- Maintenance Margin: A specific amount of funds, less than the initial margin, needed to maintain an open futures position

- Margin Call: A request from the broker for the customer to deposit additional funds to reestablish initial margin levels, or to liquidate a position after the value of the position drops below the maintenance margin threshold

Margin levels are set by the exchanges, but brokers can add to the minimum requirements to manage their own risk. In day trading, margin calls are rare, because the idea is to close positions before the end of the trading day and end each day flat (with no open positions).

Nevertheless, let's work through a hypothetical example to see how a margin call might look.

The initial margin for one crude oil futures contract is $4,000. Since the value is $54 per barrel and 1,000 barrels underlie one contract, the contract size is $54,000, and $4,000 represents roughly 7% of the value of the contract size. The maintenance margin is $3,250.

A trader takes a long position in one contract, and, to their dismay, crude oil drops 5% the next day to $51.30. They have an unrealized loss of $2,700 ($54,000 – $51,300). Subtract that from the $4,000 initial margin, and the position has dropped to $1,300, below the $3,250 maintenance margin. A margin call is sent, and the trader must deposit more money (to restore the $4,000 initial margin) or potentially see the position liquidated.

Margin requirements vary greatly by futures contracts and are largely determined by the volatility of the underlying asset. For example, the initial margin on a Treasury note contract is a much smaller percentage of contract size than that on a crude oil contract because, on a daily percentage basis, crude oil moves a lot faster, with bigger daily percentage moves, than Treasury notes.

In terms of specific products, futures contracts can be compartmentalized into a handful of groups: metals, grains, stock indexes, financials, currencies, livestock, and energies.

o **Requirements for Trading Futures**

Other than account minimums set by the broker and margin deposits, there are no requirements for trading futures contracts. The exchanges have even created contracts to appeal to smaller investors and day traders. An example is the S&P E-mini, which is by far the most popular among the stock index futures contracts.

While not required, it is important for traders to understand key dates for futures and to trade the correct expiration months. In other words, you never want to find yourself in a position where you need to take delivery of 5,000 barrels of crude oil!

Here are some key dates:

- Expiration Day: The day the futures contract expires and ceases to exist

- First Notice Day: The first day the exchange can assign delivery on accounts with open positions

- Rollover Day: The day that traders begin trading the new contract

- Last Trading Day: The last day that a futures contract can be closed before delivery

The expiration month with the greatest volume is typically the best one to day trade.

The rollover day is important, as well. It is the day traders begin trading the new contract, and there is usually a migration where you see volume reducing in the soon-to-expire contract and volume increases in the new contract. Once I see that the new contract has more volume than the old, I begin trading the new contract.

For crude oil and the other energy futures, rollover typically takes place on or around the 18th of each month.

For example, from approximately July 18 through August 17, the September contract is traded. Around August 18, we begin trading the October contract.

This can vary depending on how the days fall on the calendar, and at times I've seen the majority of the volume migrate to the new contract as early as the 15th.

On the other hand, E-minis and currencies have contracts that trade for the entire calendar quarter (March, June, September, and December).

They typically rollover by the second Friday of the new quarter. So, for trading purposes, when the September contract ends, the December contract begins on the second Friday of September.

o **The Pros and Cons of Day Trading Futures**

The futures market has been around for centuries for one simple reason: it works. Farmers, portfolio managers, metal producers, and large manufacturers find a lot of value in futures because these contracts allow them to do things like lock-in prices, hedge risk, and manage inventories. There are large pools of liquidity in many contracts, and that is great for day traders.

The trading hours for futures are longer than for most other markets, and, while I prefer trading for a few hours (or, ideally, minutes) in the morning, there are opportunities well beyond that. At the very moment, I shorted some crude oil contracts and exited with a .12 profit, making a quick $120 per contract. The entire trade took about two minutes. Such is the life of an experienced day trader. The S&P E-mini, for example, trades almost all day during the week and is open for trading Sunday evenings at 6:00 p.m. ET.

Tick size is another important factor to consider when looking at a futures contract. It is the minimum price fluctuation for a given instrument.

In our crude oil example, one contract is 1,000 barrels, and therefore a $1 move in the crude oil price per barrel represents a $1,000 change in the value of the contract. Each move can be as small as $10 because the minimum tick size is .01 per barrel. In other words, each one-cent change in crude oil results in a $10 change in the value of the position.

Having smaller tick sizes is a boon for day traders because it creates a lot of potential price levels for entries and exits. For instance, you can buy at $54.06 with a target at $54.21 and stop-loss at $53.99. There are endless possibilities. (This is in no way an actual trading suggestion because all trades should be placed within the context of a proven trade plan.)

The costs of trading futures have come down a lot, thanks to advances in electronic platforms and competition among futures brokerages. Some brokers charge only a few dollars for trades (including exchange fees). In most liquid markets, like crude oil and stock indexes, the bid-ask spreads are narrow, which minimizes slippage as well.

One disadvantage of trading S&P E-mini (ES) futures is that the contract trades in one-quarter-point ticks. Each point is worth $50, and each tick is worth $12.50.

That is quite expensive, especially when you consider that it is so widely traded that you have a lot of other traders waiting to get filled at specific prices. It can feel like standing in line at the DMV.

Many times I have put on a trade that actually hits a target exactly, and my order does not get filled. I am literally waiting to exit my position. Then the price backs off the target price, and I am faced with a tough decision: Should I just get out as the price backs off my target, paying another tick or two in slippage? Or should I wait to see if the price comes back up and returns to my price target?

With ES, it generally has to trade through my target (move to the target price and beyond) to get filled. For instance, if my target is 2,879.25, it must trade to 2,879.50 to assure a fill.

On the other hand, if I wait and hold the position (rather than exiting it immediately), I risk the price continuing in the opposite direction, in which case all my hard work to trade up to my projected target was for naught. $12.50 per tick is expensive, and I risk giving back a larger percentage of my profit objective, on average.

Other markets are less costly, and it's easier to get filled at specific price targets. Crude oil is $10 per tick. I usually get filled right when I hit my target, but even if, for some reason, I do not, I can quickly exit the position and pay a much smaller percentage in slippage. Or, for stock indexes, the Russell E-mini (RTY) trades in ticks of one-tenth of a point. A tick is only worth $5. The percentage of my slippage costs is a much smaller percentage of my overall trade objective. Keeping costs down is essential to long-term success.

CHAPTER 2:

What is Forex?

A s we noted in the introduction, Forex means foreign exchange. This is a market where the world's currencies are traded against one another, which determines the exchange rates that are used worldwide when converting from one currency to another.

This type of currency conversion happens all the time, countless times every single day.

If you are traveling, you'll find yourself having to change dollars for Mexican Pesos, or Euros for Great British Pounds.

A business importing parts from Japan will create a situation where dollars have to be converted into Japanese Yen at some point. To use their revenues in their home country, the Japanese company will need to trade the dollars they receive for Yen.

The rates that are used for transactions like these are set on the Forex market. Like stock market prices, the exchange rates between currencies are constantly fluctuating.

One day, the dollar might be favored against the Euro, but the next day, it might be the other way around.

o __What Is the Forex Market?__

The Forex market is a bit different than the stock market if you are thinking in those terms. The first thing to note is that the Forex market is completely global. There is Forex trading in New York, London, Singapore, and Sydney. Since the trading that is taking place is global, the Forex markets are open 24 hours a day on business days.

This is exciting for small investors because starting Sunday evening when the markets in New Zealand open, you can begin trading 24 hours a day until the weekend arrives the following Friday afternoon. Understanding the impact of the many different trading centers is important, the times of transition can impact trading volume and other factors.

For example, if you are trading in the United States, you'll want to be paying attention when the trading day in New York is winding down, but trading in London is starting to get going.

The Forex market isn't only global; it's not really like NASDAQ or the New York Stock Exchange. You can think of Forex as being an over the counter market. It's very fast-paced, and that can be exciting for many people but stressful for others.

But as many different trading styles work on the stock markets, many different trading styles work on Forex. You can be a day trader on Forex, or you can swing trade. Or you could hold a position over a long time period. There are many different ways to go about trading on Forex to make profits.

But many strategies are unique to Forex, that result from the unique properties of the market and the assets being traded, and how they are being traded. Many different styles of trading can be adjusted, depending on the time commitment that you are willing or able to put into your trading.

- ## Can Forex Trading Be a Full-Time Business?

The reason that lots of people fail at Forex trading is that they take a casual approach to it that isn't going to work. They just start trading on a whim without actually putting the time into study and learn how it really works.

The second factor that causes people to fail is that they let emotion take over their trading. When you have real money on the line, it's only natural to feel emotions like panic, or elation, and even greed. But letting emotions take over your trading is a recipe for disaster. Those who can trade as if they were "Mr. Spock" are the traders who become profitable. I am warning you right from the get-go. If you let emotion rule your trades, you will fail to make profits. We will talk about some tips and explore the trading mindset so that you can avoid falling prey to this common problem.

Third, reckless trading practices like risking your entire account on one trade lead many people to fail. We will talk about good trading practices and how to minimize risk later. We will also explore ways to create a trading plan. Just like with emotion, people who create a trading plan are the ones who can make a living trading on Forex, those who trade on a whim or a series of whims either find themselves losing money, or merely breaking even. To be blunt, the choice is yours from this moment forward. All I can do is give you the advice; it's going to be up to you to get it done. If you don't fall prey to the top reasons for failure, then making a full-time living trading on Forex markets is a real possibility, even likelihood. Once you get established, then it's only a matter of consistently growing to earn profits.

o <u>Where Did Forex Come From?</u>

If you are under the age of 40, you probably feel like there has always been a Forex market. If you are over 40, then it probably seems like it came out of nowhere. So what is the story behind this?

Before the late 1990s, the currency exchange was very different. Basically, the currency exchange was not available to small investors. Back in the old days, currency exchange only went on between the big banks and large "smart money" players that were allowed in on the action. That was a very different world, and compared to today's Forex markets, it was slow and lumbering. This is called interbank trading. Transactions were settled at the end of each day, which is completely different from the way it works today.

The 1990s was an explosive decade. The internet was "invented," and this opened up a lot of opportunities for business and investing. Some smart people got together in the mid-to-late 1990s and saw an opportunity to open up Forex trading to the general public.

What they came up with was a system that set up an intermediary between the banks and the general public, using something like a middle man broker. The broker would trade with the banks, and then they would turn around and make trades with individuals. This is how the modern Forex market was born, and it's how it was opened up to individuals like us to get involved.

The intermediary or middle man between the banks and the public is called a Forex dealer, or FX Dealer for short.

Interbank trading still goes on, but trading using FX dealers had exploded since 1998 when the first dealer began operating. The way it works is pretty simple. Banks and FX dealers trade with one another. The liquidity in the system is provided by the big banks. The FX dealers then trade with small and individual traders among the general public.

o **Understanding FX Dealers**

It's important to know this as background information, but when you actually begin trading, it won't be all that important. In any case, it's actually pretty easy to understand, so let's have a deeper look at how the system works behind the scenes.

As we said, an FX dealer trades with the banks and also with the general public. There are different types of FX dealers. One type of FX dealer is called a dealing desk. The fundamental point of the dealing desk is that the dealing desk takes the other side of the trade. So if you opt to buy Euros with US Dollars, the dealing desk sells you the Euros. In the early days, this was a conflict of interest, but in today's markets, this runs very smoothly and fairly, and there are other types of dealers as well.

The other type is called straight-through processing, or STP. This is an FX dealer that operates more like a stock brokerage. That is, when you put in a trade, an STP dealer finds another trader to take the other side of the position. That can be an individual trader, or it could even be a bank. But the dealer does not take the other side of the trade.

As the markets have evolved, the price differences between the two methods have become minimal to non-existent. So you shouldn't be concerned about any conflict of interest in doing business with a dealing desk, the trade is going to be the same either way as far as practical matters are concerned.

Typically, large trades don't work well with an STP. We are talking about trades on the order of a million dollars per trade and up. Those large trades are going to go through a dealing desk, because finding an individual trader willing to take the trade would be a time-consuming process. To keep the market liquid and running smoothly, running large trades like that through a dealing desk makes sense. Think of it as the "market maker" on the options markets, who will take the other side of a trade, if necessary, to keep the markets liquid and smooth.

Small trades (which can seem quite large to us individual investors) work well with STP forex dealers. So chances are this is what you're going to be dealing with if you are trading less than a million dollars per trade. If you are trading hundreds or thousands of dollars at a time, my bet is you're more than likely dealing with STP, and another individual is taking the other side of the trade.

o **Pros of Forex**

There are many benefits to trading in forex markets.

▪ **Liquidity**

The first and most important benefit of forex trading is its liquidity. As you know, the forex market is extremely liquid, meaning you can sell your currency at any time. There will be a lot of takers for it, as they will be looking to buy a particular currency. The highly liquid market can help you avoid any loss as you don't have to wait on your currency to be sold. And all of it is automatic. You only have to give the sell order, and within no time, your entire order will be sold.

▪ **Easy to Modify**

Forex Trading markets put no restrictions on how much money a forex trader can use. Forex traders can trade a variety of goods and services.

Besides, the forex market does not have many rules and regulations for the forex trader to follow. The regulations that exist guide forex traders on when to enter and when to exit a trade.

- **Individual Control**

Nobody controls the foreign market. Therefore, a forex trader has complete autonomy concerning making a trade. The forex market regulates itself and levels the playing field.

There are no intermediaries involved — a forex trader trades directly in the open forex market, and a retail forex broker eases that process.

- **Lucidity of Information**

The Forex Trading market gives information straightforwardly to the public about the rates and price movement forecasts. The forex market traders have free and equal access to the market's information, and that makes it easy for the traders to make calculated and risk-free trading decisions.

Forex traders also have access to past information that helps in analyzing the market tendencies and forecasting the direction, which the market will take.

- **Widespread Options**

The forex market provides a variety of options to forex investors. As a result, forex investors can take advantage of the available options to trade in different currencies in pairs.

An investor has the option of getting into foreign exchange spot trade or trading in currency futures to make the most of his or her investment.

- **Money-Making Gains**

The forex market provides Forex Trading measures that guard against financial loss. To ensure that a forex trader maximizes of gaining profits, the forex market has provisions for minimizing loss through making stop-loss orders.

Stop-loss orders enable forex traders to determine the closing price of their trade and thereby avoiding unforeseen losses.

- **24-Hour Market**

Foreign exchange markets remain open for 24-hours a day and 6 days a week. That means that the market stays open most of the time, and it is not subject to external factors that may affect it.

Consequently, forex traders are flexible to work during the hours that suit them best.

- **Low Operation Costs**

Operation costs in the forex currency markets are competent in trading in the forex market. The cost of operation in the currency market is in the form of spreads measured in pips. A pip is the fourth place after the decimal point of a percent.

For example, is the selling price was 2.5887, and the buying price was 2.5889, then the transaction cost is 2pips. Brokers may charge commissions on a fraction of the amount of the trade.

- **Chief Financial Market**

The forex market is the biggest financial market in the world. That is because global corporations and big financial institutions participate dynamically in the foreign exchange market.

The foreign exchange market empowers major financial institutions to retail stockholders to seek out profits from currency variations connected to the global economy.

- **One Can Use the Leverage**

The forex markets allow forex traders to capitalize on the advantage. Leveraging enables forex traders to be able to open positions for thousands of dollars while investing small amounts of money.

For example, when a forex trader trades at 40:1 leverage, he or she can trade $40 for every $1 that was in his or her account. That means that the forex trader can manage the trade of $40,000 for every $1,000 of investment.

- **Flexible Trading Hours**

Forex trade takes five and a half days in trading. It starts from Sunday from 9.00 pm to Friday at 10.00 pm, Greenwich Mean Time. When a major center in one comes to an end, there is always another center open. Since forex trade is not central pointed, but over the counter, it gives traders flexibility in trading. A trader does not have to wait for a closed session to start so that he can trade. He can always trade with the open, active sessions during the trading hours.

Traders should note that, despite the flexibility in trading hours of the foreign exchange, the opening hours of the markets sometimes vary, especially in March, April, October, and November. The reason for the variation in opening hours is because the different countries shift differently on daylight saving. It is crucial for retail traders also to understand that during the weekend, they are not allowed to trade. All markets in the forex market close on Friday at 10.00 pm, United Kingdom Time, and opens on Sunday evening at 9.00 pm, United Kingdom Time.

The lack of trading on the weekend of the forex market can cause a difference in the prices. The difference between Friday when the prices close and Sunday when the prices open is called a gap. This gap can be an increase in prices in the forex market or a decrease in the prices. This means traders should be very keen on the trading hours of the weekend and change their positions according to the trend. Not being aware of this puts a trader's position at the gapping risk.

- ▪ **No or Low Commissions**

Everyone wants to save money, no matter how little it is. Forex trading gives you a chance to save some money that you could have used to by the commissions to brokers of other businesses. Forex trading has meager commissions charged by the forex traders compared to other trade brokers. When the dealers do not involve the brokers, there are commission charges, and there are also no clearance fees making the trade the better option to trade.

- **Trade More Currency Pairs**

Different variety of currency pairs is traded in forex trading. The trading of these pairs speculates on the world's events and how strong the major and the minor economies are around the world.

- **Control over the trade**

Since there are a variety of currency pairs to trade with, the trader controls what he wants to trade in without any force. The trader assesses the risks and the potential returns himself and makes a decision solely on whether to enter the trade or not. The power of trading lies entirely in the trader's hands.

- **Allows Practice**

Unlike most trades, forex trade has a demo account. This demo account helps a trader practice on how to analyze the trend and how to invest their money. Forex trading demo account equips the trader with enough knowledge and skills of the forex market before the real deal. It helps the trader make a clear decision of whether to join the trade or not. It is like being given an exam paper with a leakage.

- **Information Transparency**

You must have come across trades that hide some information and take it as an advantage to get more returns. Forex trading is the total opposite of these other trades. In forex trading, despite being a broad market has the fairest information transparency. With the market size, the fire trade makes sure that the information reaches the traders, maybe not on the exact time but the required time because of the difference in the time zones.

- **Risk-Free Demos**

Demo accounts that a trader uses for his practice are free and do not affect your money in any way. The money in the demo account can all be lost without any effect on your money. The demo account helps those who want to know what the trade entails practically before getting into it. The risk here is zero.

o **Cons of Forex**

- **Risky**

Although people who engage in forex trading are in it for the profit that they can make, the unfortunate truth is that many of these traders end up losing their investment. It is risky to participate in forex, especially if you do not know what you are doing. In fact, if you do not have knowledge of forex and simply jump in without preparation, it is most likely that you will suffer a big loss in just a few days. If you get too careless, then you can expect to lose your money on the very first day of trading.

Even those who have been trading for years are still careful before they open a position. As a beginner, you need to be more cautious of your actions.

Although you are well encouraged to do all the necessary research and analysis before making any trade, there is no amount of preparation that can guarantee 100% it will give you a favorable outcome. Literally, every trade that you make has its risks.

- **Lower return**

You can indeed make lots of money with forex even if you just invest a small amount since you can use the power leverage. It is also true that trading currencies have a higher profit potential than just investing in stocks.

However, forex trading is not the one that offers the highest payout. Of you want a higher return, then you might want to consider options trading instead of forex trading. With options trading, you can get as high as a 90% return for every trade that lasts as fast as two minutes or even less.

However, it is worth noting that options trading is so much riskier than forex trading. Options trading is like gambling in the casino. There is also no way to leverage your position.

- **Volatility**

The prices of different currencies are affected by many factors. The forex market can, from time to time, be highly volatile. You can also expect some unforeseeable events to take place. The bad part is that traders may not be able to do anything about them when they occur.

For example, during the time when Iceland got bankrupt, forex traders holding Icelandic krona could not do anything but watch how they were holding something that has significantly depreciated. This is unlike in investing in stocks where shareholders can somehow pressure the board of directors to act more promptly and take appropriate actions. To avoid being a victim of the high volatility of the market, it is well-advised that you limit your losses and always be sure to use a well-planned approach when trading.

- **Less regulated**

Since forex trading is not regulated by any central authority, traders usually rely on their broker to facilitate a trade. If you get lucky and end up working with an unreliable broker, you will only get scammed and cheated in the process. Also, since you will be relying on the assistance extended to you by a broker, you may not have total control over your trades and orders.

Therefore, to prevent this from happening, it is important that you only work with regulated and legitimate brokers. Since forex takes place in an over-the-counter market, you need to be careful in choosing your broker.

- **Self-taught**

Unlike investing in stocks where you can ask for assistance from trade advisors and portfolio managers, dealing with forex is ultimately something that you do on your own. It is not a surprise for beginners to lose their initial investment.

Unfortunately, after experiencing a bad loss, they usually get discouraged, which prevents them from fully learning the ins and outs of trading. Hence, when you are just starting out, you must admit to yourself that you are just a newbie.

As much as possible, take advantage of the demo account that is provided to you by your broker, so that you can familiarize yourself with the actual trading environment. It is also advised that you start out small even if you have a big amount of money that ready for trading in your account.

- **Hard to predict**

Multiple factors affect the forex market. In fact, this is the reason why forex traders usually rely on technical analysis. With so many factors that influence the prices of the different currencies, it becomes almost impossible to predict the price movement of a currency. Of course, you can always apply an effective strategy, but it does not change the fact that the forex market is hard, if not impossible, to predict.

CHAPTER 3:

How Prices Are Determined

O ptions prices are determined in part by the price of the underlying stock. But options prices are also influenced by the time left to expiration and some other factors.

We are going to go over all the different ways that the price of a given option can change and what will be behind the changes.

It's important to have a firm grasp of these concepts so that you don't go into options as a naïve beginning trader.

Pricing is a complex subject when it comes to options trading. Not only is the price of an option based on the value of the asset, but other external factors have influence.

As an options trader, you want to make sure that you maximize your efforts to make a profit.

Learning how to determine the prices, you should pay for options is one of the basic ways that you can ensure that your yield is as high as it can be.

You do not want to be stiffed by paying higher premiums than you should.

The pricing of options is determined by several factors. Each will be stated below.

▪ The Value of the Asset

The effect this has on options prices is straightforward. If the value of this asset goes down, then exercising the option to sell becomes more valuable, while the right to buy is becoming less valuable.

On the other hand, if the value increases, the right to sell it becomes less valuable, while the right to buy it becomes more appealing due to this increase.

▪ The Intrinsic Value

When an options trader pays a premium, this sum represents two values. The premium is made up of the intrinsic value, which is the current value of the option and the potential increase in value that this option can obtain over time.

This potential increase over time is known as the time value.

We are discussing the intrinsic value. The intrinsic value is how much money the option is currently worth. It represents what the buyer would receive if he or she decided to exercise the option at the current time.

Intrinsic value is calculated by determining the difference in the current price of an asset and a strike price of the option.

For an option to have an intrinsic value of zero, the option must be out of money. Therefore, the buyer would not exercise the option because this would result in a loss. The common strategy here is allowing the option to expire so that no pay off is made. As a result, the intrinsic value results in nothing to the buyer.

For a buyer to be in the money, the intrinsic value has to be greater than the premium to increase the value of the option. This places the buyer in a position to make a profit. The intrinsic value of for in the money for call options and put options are calculated slightly differently. The formulas are as follows:

- **The Time Value**

This value is the additional amount an investor is willing to contribute to the premium of an option in addition to the intrinsic value. This willingness stems from the belief that an option will increase in value before the expiration date reaches.

Typically, an investor is only willing to put forth this extra amount if the option expires months away.

There would be little to no change in the value of an option in a few days.

The time value is calculated by finding the difference between the intrinsic value of an option and the premium. The formula looks like this:

- Option Premium - Intrinsic Value = Time Value

Therefore, the total price of an option premium follows this formula:

- Intrinsic Value + Time Value = Option Premium

Both time value and intrinsic value help traders understand the value of what they are paying for if they decide to purchase an option.

While the intrinsic value represents the worth of the option if the buyer were to exercise it at the current time, the time value represents the possible future value before or on the expiration date. These two values are important because they help traders understand the risk versus the reward of considering an option.

- **Volatility**

This describes how likely a price change will occur during a specified amount of time on the financial market. If a financial market is nonvolatile, then the prices change very slowly or remain totally unaffected over a specific amount of time. Volatile markets, on the other hand, have fast-changing prices over short periods of time.

Options traders can make use of a financial market's volatility to get a higher yield for their investment in the future.

Options traders normally avoid slow-changing financial markets because these non-volatile markets often mean that no potential profit is available to the trader. Therefore, options traders thrive on volatility even though volatility increases the risk of option trading.

As a result, an options trader needs to know how to read the financial market correctly to know which options are likely to yield the highest returns. This ability comes with experience, continuous learning, and keeping up to date on the happenings of the financial markets.

Many factors affect the volatility of the financial market. These factors include politics, national economics, and news reports. Options traders typically use one of two options strategies to gain the best yield from volatile markets. They are called a straddle strategy and the strangle strategy.

o __Implied Volatility__

One of the most important characteristics of options after considering delta and time decay is the amount a stock price varies with time. Volatility will give you an idea of how will the price swings of stock are. If you look at a stock chart, I am sure that you are used to seeing the price go up and down a lot, giving a largely jagged curve.

The more that it fluctuates, and the bigger the fluctuations in price, the higher the volatility. Of course, everything is relative, and so you can't say that any stock has an "absolute" level of volatility.

What is done is the volatility for the entire market is calculated, and then the volatility of a stock is compared to the volatility of the market as a whole. When looking at the stocks themselves, this is given by a quantity called beta.

If the stock generally moves with the stock market at large, beta is positive. If beta is 1.0, that means that it has the same volatility as the entire market. That is a stock with average volatility.

If beta is less than 1.0, then the stock doesn't have much volatility. The amount below 1.0 tells you how much less volatile the stock is in comparison to the market as a whole. So, if the beta is given as 0.7, this means that the stock is 30% less volatile than the market average.

If beta is greater than 1.0, then the stock is more volatile than the average. If you see a stock with a beta of 1.42, that means the stock is 42% more volatile than the average for the market. If beta is negative, that means the stock, on average, moves against the market. When the market goes up, it goes down and vice versa.

Most stocks don't have a negative beta, but they are not hard to find either. Volatility is a dynamic quantity, so when you look it up, you are looking at a snapshot of the volatility at that given moment.

Of course, under most circumstances, it's not likely to change very much over short periods like a few weeks or a month. There are exceptions to this, including earnings season.

Implied volatility is a quantity that is given for options. Implied volatility is a measure of the coming volatility that the stock price is expected to see over the lifetime of the option (that is until the expiration date).

One of the things that make options valuable is the probability that the price of the stock will move in a direction that is favorable to the strike price. When an option goes in the money, or deeper in the money (that is the share price moves even higher relative to the strike price of a call, or lower relative to the strike price of a put), the value of the option can increase by a large margin.

If a stock is more volatile, there is more chance of this happening, since the price is going to be going through larger price swings. Therefore, the higher the implied volatility, the higher the price of the option.

In the following, we will consider a hypothetical situation to illustrate. This time, we will look at an option that would have a strike price that was set to a hundred dollars and a $100 share price, so the option is exactly at the money. Here are the prices that you would see for some different values of implied volatility:

- Implied volatility = 40%: Option price is $562.

- Implied volatility = 20%: Option price is $282

- Implied volatility = 10%: Option price is $142

- Implied volatility = 80%: Option price is $1,119

That is for a call option.

As you can see, implied volatility has quite a large influence on the price of an option. For this reason, professional options traders look at implied volatility just as much as they look to the comparison between the strike price and the market stock price. One way to make profits is to seek out options that have high implied volatility.

Each quarter, companies report their earnings. This is one time when implied volatility is going to be really important. As mentioned earlier, earnings calls can send the price of a stock up or down by a large amount. Prices can move $10, $20, or $40 a share in one direction or the other depending on whether the earnings call beat expectations or not, and whether or not there was a piece of good or bad news thrown in with the earnings report. In other words, this is a highly volatile situation.

This offers opportunities for profits. The way that professional traders handle this is they purchase options on companies that are going to have upcoming earnings calls.

Typically, you might purchase options about a week ahead of the earnings call. At that time, the implied volatility is going to be relatively low. It may be in the range of 15-20%.

As time passes and it gets closer to the earnings call, implied volatility will go up by a lot. In fact, for the examples above, it was no accident that I selected implied volatility of 80%.

Recently, I noticed that the implied volatility on some Tesla options shot up to 82%. As the implied volatility goes up, the value of the option increases, providing an opportunity for profits.

o **Option Pricing Models**

Option pricing theory uses all of the variables mentioned above to theoretically calculate the value of an option.

It is a tool that allows trainers to get an estimate of an option's fair value as they incorporate different strategies to maximize profitability. Luckily, there are models that traders can use to implement option pricing strategies to their advantage. Three commonly used pricing models for option values are:

- The Black-Scholes Model

- Binomial Option Pricing Model

- Monte-Carlo Simulations

- **The Black Scholes Model**

Commonly known as the Black-Scholes-Merton (BSM) model was designed by the three economists, Fischer Black, Robert Merton and Myron Scholes in 1973. Originally used to price European options (meaning the option can only be exercised on the expiration date), this is a mathematical system that has a huge influence on modern option pricing. The pricing model helps differentiate options from gambling by determining the option premium to be paid reasonably. It calculates the return on the income the investor is likely to earn less the amount paid.

As this is primarily used to determine a European call option, the formula used to calculate it looks like this:

- $SN(d1) - Xe - rt\ N(d2) = $ Call Option Premium

The letter representations in this equation stand for:

- S – Current asset price

- N – A normal distribution
- X – Strike price
- r – risk-free interest rate
- t – the time of maturity

While this pricing system is great, it does have limitations. One of these limitations is that it assumes that factors like volatility and risk-free interest will remain constant, which is not the case in actuality. It also does not factor in other costs in setting up the option.

- **Binomial Option Pricing Model**

More commonly used to develop pricing for American options, this pricing system was developed in 1979. Even as popular as the Black Scholes Model is, this model is even more frequently used in practice because it is more intuitive.

This pricing system allows for the assumption that there are two possible outcomes – one where the outcome moves up and one where the outcome moves down.

This system differs from the Black Scholes Model in the way that it allows calculations for multiple periods, whereas the Black Scholes Model does not. This advantage gives a multi-period view, which is very advantageous to options traders. This model makes use of binomial trees to figure out options pricing. These are diagrams with the main formula branching off into two different directions. This branching off is what gives the multi-period view that this pricing system is famous for. For this pricing system to work, the following assumptions are made:

- There are 2 possible prices for the associated asset, hence the name of the pricing system. Bi means 2.
- The 2 possibilities involve the price of the asset moving up or down.
- No dividends are being paid on the asset.
- The rate of interest does not change through the life of the option
- There are no risks attached to the transaction.
- There are no other costs associated with the option.

Clearly, just like with the Black Scholes Model, there is some limitation with those assumptions. Still, the pricing system is highly valuable in the valuing of American options since such options can be exercised any time until the expiration date.

▪ Monte Carlo Simulations

Used in multiple fields across the board like science, engineering, and finance, this model allows the options trader to consider multiple outcomes due to the involvement of random factors. It allows for the consideration of risk and unpredictability, unlike the first two pricing models. This is why it is also sometimes called multiple probability simulation.

- **A Final Word on Pricing**

The reason I went into such depth on pricing options is that I want you to realize that everything related to options requires careful consideration right down to the premiums paid.

This needs to be a fair trade for all the parties involved, and premium pricing needs to reflect that fairness. When considering the options premium, remember to search deeper than the surface level to ensure that fairness and to ensure that you are gaining the profit that you need out of the transaction.

o **Interest Rates**

Most people are familiar with the term interest rates. Interest rates apply to mortgages bank accounts and more. Interest rates, as it applies to option trading, is slightly different from the common variations.

The interest rate is defined as the percentage of a particular rate for the use of money lent over a while. This interest rate of an option has different effects on the call option and put option.

The premiums for call options rise when interest rates rise and fall when interest rates fall. The effect is the opposite on puts options. The premiums for put options fall when interest rates rise and rise when interest rates fall.

Interest rates affect the time value of options no matter what category they fall in!

You will come across the term risk-free interest rate many times in your study of options trading. This is described as the return made on an investment with no loss of capital.

This is a misleading term because all investments carry some level of risk, no matter how minute. This more serves as a parameter in options pricing models such as the Black-Scholes model to determine the premium that should be paid.

- **Volume and Open Interest**

Volume is a measure of how many times that option was traded on the current (if the markets are open) or previous trading days.

Volume and open interest are not going to be factors you consider when trading an option. However, you also need to consider how difficult it's going to be when exiting a position.

If you sell to open, you might need to buy the option back as part of your strategy. If you buy an option, you want to be able to sell it quickly in order to take profits at a level that you're comfortable with.

Some options might look appealing on the surface, but if you can't buy and sell them quickly, they might be more trouble than they are worth. So, you want the trading activity to be taking place at a reasonable level.

Open interest will tell you the number of option contracts that are out there on the market. This is for a single strike price. It would also be for the same expiration date and one type of option.

So, if I have a Tesla call option, consider the possibilities. Suppose that there is a strike price of $250 that expires on August 2, I can look at the open interest to see how many of these contracts are on the market.

Generally speaking, you want the open interest to be 100 or higher. For some highly traded securities, the open interest can be in the thousands. This is a dynamic quantity; it will change if more traders sell to open.

But the rule of thumb is that 100 or higher gives you enough action on that contract that you can buy or sell later without having to wait a terribly long time to close the position.

If open interest is really low, you might not find a buyer or seller at all.

- **Risk-Free Rate**

You are also going to see the risk free rate quoted for an option. This is the interest rate that you could earn on an ideal safe investment.

Generally speaking, this would be the interest you could earn from a 10-year U.S. treasury over the time period of the option. In normal times, this is an important factor to consider.

Rising interest rates (that is significantly rising) can lower the value of options. In recent years, interest rates have been very low, and changes in interest rates have been small and very conservative. So at the present time at least, this is not really something to worry about.

- **Dividends**

Dividends are distributions of portions of a company's profit at a specified period. This distribution must be decided and managed by the board of directors of a company. It is paid to a specific group of shareholders. These dividends can be distributed in the form of cash, shares of stock, and other types of property. Exchange-traded funds and mutual funds also pay out dividends.

As it relates to options trading, options do not actually pay dividends. However, the associated assets attached to that option can have them. Thus, an options trader can receive those dividends if he or she exercises that option and takes ownership of those particular assets. While both call and put options can be affected by the presence of dividends of the associated asset, this effect on the types of options is widely varied. While the presence of dividends makes call options less expensive due to the anticipation of a drop in price, it makes put options more expensive because the price will be decreased by the amount of the dividend.

CHAPTER 4:

Strike Price and Time Decay

o **Strike Price**

The strike price is one of the most important if not the most important thing to understand when it comes to option contracts. The strike price will determine whether the underlying stock is actually bought or sold at or before the expiration date. When evaluating any options contract, the strike price is the first thing that you should look at. It's worth reviewing the concept and how it's utilized in the actual marketplace.

The strike price will let you home in on the profits that can be made on an options contract. It's the break-even point but also gives you an idea as to your profits and losses. Of course, the seller always gets the premium no matter what.

For a call contract, the strike price is the price that must be exceeded by the current market price of the underlying equity. For example, if the strike price is $100 on a call contract, and the current market price goes to any price above $100, then the purchaser of the call can exercise their right at any time to buy the stock. Then the stock can be disposed of with a profit. Suppose that the current price rises to $130. Then you can exercise your option to buy the stock at $100 a share, and then turn around and sell it on the market for $130 a share, making a $30 profit per share before taking into account the premium and other fees that might accrue with your trades. While as the buyer of the contract, you have no obligations other than paying the premium, the seller is obligated no matter what, and they must sell you the shares at $100 per share no matter how much it pains them to see the $130 per share price. Of course, there are reasons behind the curtain that will explain why they would bother entering this kind of arrangement.

For a put contract, the strike price likewise plays a central role, but the value of the stock relative to the strike price works oppositely. A put is a bet that the underlying equity will decrease in value by a certain amount.

Hence if the stock price drops below the strike price, then the buyer can exercise their right to sell the shares at the strike price even though the market price is lower. So, if your price is $100, if the current price of the equity drops to $80, the seller obligated to buy the 100 shares per contract from you at $100 a share even though the market price is $80 per share. In this case, you've made a gross profit of $20 a share.

The value of the strike price will not only tell you profitability but give you an indication of how much the stock must move before you can exercise your rights.

Often when the amount is smaller, you might be better off. When you know the strike price of different options contracts, then you can evaluate which one is better for you to buy. Suppose that a stock is currently trading at $80, and you find two options to put contracts. One has a strike price of $75, and the other has a strike price of $60. Further, let's suppose that both contracts expire at the same time. In the first case, the stock price in the market will need to drop just $5 before the contract becomes profitable. For the second contract, it will have to drop $20.

The potential worth of each contract per share is the difference. For the contract with the $75 strike price, that is only $5. For the second contract with the strike price of $60, the potential worth is $20, four times as much.

Determining which contract is better is a matter of analysis and taking some risk. You can't just go by face value. Still, you must take into consideration the expiration date together with an analysis of what the stock will actually do over that time period.

It may be that it's going to be impossible for the stock to drop $20 to make the second contract valuable. If the expiration date comes before the stock drops that much in price, the contract will be worthless. In other words, you'd never be able to exercise your option of selling shares at the strike amount.

On the other hand, even though there is not much discrepancy between the strike and the market amount for the first contract, and the market price might only drop to say $70 per share, the chances of this happening before the expiration date is more likely.

Your analysis might be different if the contract with the lower strike price has a longer expiration date. The lesson to take to heart is that a stock is more likely to move by smaller amounts over short periods. But the higher the risk, the more the potential profits.

o **Time Decay**

If an option is valued so that it is the same as the share price, or if it is out of the money, time decay is going to have a significant influence over the value of an option at any given time. For an option that can be said to be in the money, the influence of time decay is going to be much less. The closer you get to the expiration date; the time value exerts less influence on the overall price of the option.

In that case, it's going to be more influenced by implied volatility and the underlying share price. To take an example, at four days to expiration, a $100 strike price on an underlying stock when the market price is set equal to $110 per share will have $10 in intrinsic value with $0.56 in extrinsic value and a total price per share of $10.56. So the price is heavily weighted to the underlying price of the shares.

However, theta is -0.23, meaning that on a per-share basis, at market open the following day, the option will lose $0.23 in value, all other things being equal. Of course, all other things are not equal, and changes in share price and implied volatility may wipe that out or add to it.

The important thing to do is check theta every afternoon so you can estimate what the cost is going to be for holding the option overnight. Time decay is an exponential phenomenon, so it decays faster the closer you get to the expiration date. The important path for the trader is knowing when other factors are going to be more important than time decay, you are not simply going to sell off your option because it's going to lose value from time decay the following morning.

As you know, time decay has a very strong impact on the valuation of premiums. This is one of the most important indicators that you must keep in mind. This Greek symbol represents the time value in the contract or its extrinsic value.

It is also important to keep in mind that although there is a consistent time decay in the contract, the rate of decay is always not steady.

There are several key factors like the volatility, performance, OI, that may affect the time decay. However, one thing is certain that the value of theta would start going down rapidly in the contract, and by the last day, it would become zero as there would be no time value left in the stock.

o **Bull vs. Bear Markets**

The terms bull market and bear market are commonly used by traders and investors and throughout the financial world. Not all who use these terms or hear them understand exactly what they mean. Yet they are crucial and affect our trading strategies and plans.

As a trader, you can expect to hear these two terms used a lot, and you must understand what they mean as well as the crucial similarities and differences.

- **Bull Markets**

A bull market is a market that trends upwards for a given period of time. The markets are mostly on such a trend most of the time. The trend may start after a period of decline, followed by stability. An upward trend in the market means that stock prices are on the rise, the economy is doing well, and the outlook is generally positive. As such, more and more traders and investors seek to invest their money during this period. There are a number of factors that result in a bull market. These are low-interest rates, a booming or strong economy, high employment rates, and great government policies that support growth. Under such circumstances, the bull market will enjoy a long run, and both traders and investors will thrive.

- **Bear Markets**

A bear market is the exact opposite of a bull market. The market trends downwards, and stock prices fall. An observer would say that the market movement is moving in a downward direction quarter after quarter. When quantified, a bear market loses ground by about twenty percent. This means the trend tends negatively with a 20% loss each quarter. Certain factors cause bear markets. One of these is a lack of employment, and another is a poorly performing economy. A successful economy is one where employment rates are high, and interest rates are low. On the other hand, a poorly performing economy is one where interest rates are high, there are fewer than desired jobs, and government policies are unfriendly towards businesses. Bear markets cause a lot of worry and concern in a lot of people, especially traders and investors. Many take out their investments from the markets from fear of losing out. As such, depression tends to set in, and the economy starts to underperform. There are reasons why the terms bull market and bear market are used. A bull attacks by striking upwards hence the term bull for a market that's headed upwards. A bear attacks by swiping downwards towards its victim during an attack. This is why the term bear market is used. The markets tend to experience bull runs most of the time, which are followed by brief bear markets less than 30 percent of the time.

- **Objective**

You have to be very specific when it comes to the objective that you have for that investment you are considering: Is it to speculate on a bullish or bearish view of the underlying asset or is to hedge possible risk on the stock in where you have an important position? Are you merely doing it to earn extra income? Whatever your objective is, make sure that you shed clarity on the same as it will help you in the process of making those option trades soon.

CHAPTER 5:

Best Demo Simulator & How to Use It

Investing in the stock market, as the experts point out, requires substantial knowledge and experience to control the risk and make the appropriate decisions at the right time.

That is why a virtual stock market simulator can become a fundamental tool to start trading with securities eliminating the dangers one can't afford much with one's hard-earned capital.

These simulators generally offer very advanced interfaces, a virtual economic fund to invest, and real-time information. That is to say, they have all the tools and functions necessary to learn how to invest in an online stock market as if we were in the stock market itself.

Many of these computer programs belong to banks and brokers specialized in the stock market or markets such as Forex (such as Plus500).

These applications, from our point of view, are more complete than the simple stock market games that we have found in the market for decades or than the apps that have overwhelmingly increased in recent years.

Most offer free demo accounts, although in some cases, we can find companies that request a small payment in exchange for using their platform. A small expense that is worth taking on and that can save us many dislikes in the future.

- ■ **Why Use a Bag Simulator?**

Investing in the stock market is not especially difficult, but it is essential to have good knowledge to avoid greater evils. If you want to achieve high profitability, you have to take risks, but doing it blindly can be a real disaster for our pocket. It can be suicidal, financially speaking.

That is why it is essential to train previously in everything related to the markets and their operation. For this, you can go to the editorial fund of the National Commission of the Stock Market or the Madrid Stock Exchange, where we can find practical guides and handy tips for beginners and more advanced investors.

Having the advice of an expert is also a guarantee, but if you prefer to take the road alone, we recommend that you settle the bases well before playing with real money. The risk, as we have repeated, is high if it is operated without the necessary knowledge. The stock market is not a lottery that can make you rich by investing a few euros, so you should know all the mechanisms of the market entirely to understand where and when to put your money.

In this learning process, a good stock market simulator plays an essential role. With these tools, you can play with fictitious money, see how your decisions affect your income statement, and, most importantly, create solid pillars to leap to the real world of investments. Another advantage is that the companies that offer these simulators allow you to directly operate with real money from the same or similar platform, so you will already be familiar with the interface. In many cases, it is only necessary to convert your demo account into a real account and make an income, without changing the program.

- **Pay for a bag simulator?**

Many people are wondering what the best free bag simulator for beginners is.

It is true that in the market, we can find compelling tools that do not require the payment of any amount, but it is also true that skimping on this section can be a real mistake.

Creating a CFD bag simulator that offers guarantees entails a considerable programming expense and high operating costs. That is why some companies ask for a small subscription in exchange for their use that does not usually reach 10 euros per month.

A minimum amount for a tool that tells you how to learn to invest in the stock market from home, and that allows you to practice with all the guarantees; it's worth it by any standards, of course.

Also, it is widespread that with that small fee, the user has access to manuals, tutorials, webinars, and other teaching materials to support the practical part with theoretical foundations.

Investing in the stock market in the short term is not recommended, so all this material can be of high relevance to fix concepts.

- **The Best Bag Simulators**

Once this preamble has been completed, we will analyze five of the most exciting simulators in the market. All are backed by companies with ample experience in the sector (they are banks or brokers) and are well above in quality and performance of simple stock games (we do not recommend using these games as part of your training). This listing is sorted alphabetically.

- **Active Trade**

This real-time stock market simulator offers users an account with 100,000 virtual euros so they can practice without fear of losing their money. It has personalized support and, most importantly, with courses and trading programs taught by professional traders.

With this tool, you can create your strategy, control your investments, find the companies that best fit your profile, and get detailed information on more than 18,400 shares. Essential functions to create your profile as an investor and locate those opportunities that you can take advantage of in the real world.

- **IG Spain**

The demo account of this stock market simulator allows you to invest in an online stock market in a risk-free environment. This free account has a virtual fund of 20,000 euros and offers graphics and prices in real-time. Also, you can check from your mobile or tablet to continue operating anywhere, even if you don't have a computer. The interface can be customized to suit your tastes and your style. This demo account, however, does not offer all the functionality of the real platform. The most notable differences are the following:

- Transactions made through the demo account are not subject to slippage, interest or dividend adjustments, or price movements out of the negotiation.

- Transactions can be rejected if you do not have enough funds to open them, but they will not be denied due to size or price issues.

- The graphics packages have no cost.

- The positions will not be closed if you do not have enough funds to cover the margin or current losses, something that does happen in a real account.

- **Orey iTrade**

Another easy-to-use bag simulator is that of Orey iTrade. With this tool, you will learn to invest in both the Spanish selective, that is, in the IBEX 35, as in other critical global exchanges. All online and free, since you can try it without cost and obligation.

Through its interface, you can access stock quotes in real-time and different analyses, comparative, and graphical tools. The account begins with a virtual fund of 100,000 euros to start investing.

- ## Société Générale

This trading simulator seems to us one of the most interesting since it will allow you to delve into the world of warrants, something that is not available in most of the free tools. The simulator of this French bank makes available to its users 10,000 fictitious euros to negotiate on the listed products of Société Générale and test their investment strategy without risk.

To start operating, you must register on the website www.sgbolsa.es. Registration is free. Also, the entity usually raffles gifts such as mobile phones or tablets among its new users, one more argument to try the Market Simulator, as they call it. To use the system, follow these steps:

- Register on the website www.Warrants.com.

- Connect to the website www.Warrants.com or the simulator using the e-mail and the registration password.

- Access the simulator from the Tools menu of the website www.Warrants.com.

- ## TraderTwit

The TraderTwit simulator catches our attention since it has enormous educational value. It is not free (although it is cheap), but instead offers training and a compelling platform. They have a lot of news from the sector, an exciting collaborative platform, and thousands of interactive analyses.

We like what they call "the challenge."

It is something like a 50-level training program that puts users in challenges to move from level to level. In each of them, you have to follow instructions, such as the maximum lever that can be used or the maximum loss streak.

There are also objectives to be achieved.

Based on these criteria, the user can carry out operations of buying and selling currencies, indices, or raw materials — an excellent way to learn while having fun and competing against other users in the community.

Also, the best usually takes real prizes.

o <u>**The Rules Used in Option Trading**</u>

What are the guidelines to follow in options trading? What are the rules?

These are essential questions new traders should be able to answer correctly.

We will go through the rules that you should follow in options trading. And by the end of this topic, you will have the knowledge needed to trade efficiently.

For a new emerging trader, these rules will be an eye-opener, while for an experienced options trader, it will be as a reminder.

These rules won't be a get-rich tip, and the rules will help you stay out of trouble, increase your capital, and improve your money with options.

Here are some of the rules used on options trading:

- **Don't be emotional.** The market doesn't care what you think; one of the ways to be successful in trading is not to be emotional. Don't allow your emotions to lead you, the opinions or thoughts on the market.

- **Trade small positions.** When you get into the market, it's obvious to assume the worse. It only makes sense to make smaller trades and avoid big trades to reduce the risk of losing a significant amount of the money you had invested. The best tip is to make lots of small positions because if you make just one large, you risk being knocked out when you hit a loss. About 90% of options traders do not succeed because they trade large position sizes. Trading over 5% is considered a large position, and the trader risk affecting their accounts from a bad loss.

- **Have a high trade count.** By knowing your estimated percentage chance of success, you will make a lot of trades. The higher the trade count, the higher the chances of leveling out at that expected percentage. Options trading is a number game and math, and you can pinpoint your probabilities of success in a given position. You can see your percentage chance of success; however, this can be the reason for your failure as you will have the same expectation in all your trades. So, the high trade count you make, the more consistent your percentage success rate will be.

- **Balance your portfolio.** You can bet the price direction if it goes up or down when you invest in options trading. Traders tend to focus on the investment value going up; however, you have to learn how to balance your portfolio with positions going down too.

- **Trade according to your comfort level.** If you are not comfortable trading naked options or if hedged positions give you sleepless nights, then you should trade options as a speculator forming opinions and act on them accordingly. Once you are in tune with your strategies, you will realize it will be much easier for you to make money. Each strategy is unique and individual, and it might not work for all traders. By doing this, you will lower the individual's risk level.

- **Always use a model.** Failure to check the fair value of the option before it's sold or bought is one of the biggest mistakes option traders make. It can be hard, especially if you don't have an exact real-time evaluation capability. These are the basis of the strategic investment and also be aware of the bargains and the amount you are paying for the option.

- **Have enough cash reserve.** It's essential to have a lot of your investment money in cash. It might be useful for brokers as they need a margin requirement when trading. They partition some amount to cover potential losses on your position. Try to keep about 50-60% of your investment portfolio in cash.

- **Reduce commissions and fees.** Paying commissions and fees to transact and rebalance your portfolio might be crippling you. One of the ways to lower the percentage of the charges is by using low-cost ETF's. But for a beginner, you shouldn't pay any fees to invest in stocks.

o <u>Managing Options</u>

▪ How to Hold & Buy with Options

Buying options do not guarantee that they are exercised by the buyer until expiry. Besides, there are three methods of using choices.First, the buyer should hold the mature option before it expires and then purchase the underlying asset at the agreed price. Investors do this when the current market price is higher than the strike price if the commodity has risen up.

Second, sometime before it expires, the buyer merely exercises the right. This is achieved when the asset price fluctuates up and down the agreed price. If the investor assumes the price will not go any further, he/she will exercise the option immediately after a higher price than the strike price has been registered.Finally, the investor can cause the option to expire. Investors do this if the underlying asset's price continues to decline. The loss suffered by buyers is restricted only to the premium option.

▪ How to Sell with Options

Unlike investors, if the holders want to use it, option writers will sell or buy the underlying asset. Within the negotiated contract period, they will buy or sell the asset at the strike price-even if the asset's market price is greater or lower than the agreed price.

A covered call enables the writer/seller to sell his/her own underlying asset. If the customer uses the right, the call writer will sell the commodity at the agreed price. This enables the writer to receive all of the stock's benefits as well as the dividends. The only way this does not happen is when the person decides to share the shares received with the stock.

There's still the problem of the individual who doesn't completely profit from this, however. We have recovered the premium and dividend, but they have stayed out of any other potential market rising, so you should be careful before going into this.

On the other hand, an undisclosed call allows the vendor to sell the commodity he/she does not own at the outset of the deal. If the price of the underlying asset has risen sharply, and the investor wants to exercise the option, the seller will lose a lot of money. It means the seller will only have to acquire the asset at a high price to market it to the buyer. As a result of the transaction, this can cause significant risk, and it can result in the investor losing a lot of money in the purchase.

- **Watching the Market**

Traders' allowing their options to expire is a common observation. This is true for long-term markets. To make the alternative competitive, the demand must hit a level. If a trader wants to accept an alternative, he/she will evaluate the probability that a certain price will be met by the consumer. No fair deal is assured by a cheap price. Good demand and prospects mean it's going to be a good deal. If you are looking to buy a stock option, you will watch the market for a certain period of time. See the trend and see if there's a chance with that for benefit. If it is, it is time to go for it. If not, it may be best to sit out that one and not take the risk with it.

You will watch the market every day by monitoring stocks and seeing which ones are doing well and which ones are going to stay away.

- **The Average Monthly Range**

Most traders prefer to look at the premium option rather than the potential returns. While significant, they tend to focus too much on it, while ignoring the likelihood that the demand may hit and inevitably surpass the price of the attack. It is best to keep trading options straightforward in most situations. The options trader will calculate the average monthly range of the market to decide whether an option is a good trade or not. It is a figure that gives the promise of uncertainty and the probability of break-even.

They can also compare the average monthly distribution with other similar quantities of stocks. You may see a stock with a good trading opportunity, but the overall range is bad, and there is no hope of benefit. Let's presume, however, that you see one that's a little higher than the other, but you know there's a lot of potential for that product.

Continuing with the latter is safer because it can mean a potential increase in your own earnings, and it will ultimately benefit you even later as a result.

- **Using the Average Monthly Range**

The trader wants historical prices to measure the average monthly spread. If the stock is picked as the underlying asset, historically high, weak, open and close values can be restored within a certain period of time. The average monthly range includes a certain stock's daily high and low values. During the time the market fluctuates between the high and low of a given month, the average price can be easily calculated. Conservative traders use the open and close monthly values in most cases. To get the sum, which is then added up and separated by the months, the low price is subtracted from the high price during the month.

[month 1: high price - low price] + [month 2: high price - low price] + ... / (number of months)

A trader should generally consider twice the length of the position to arrive at the time frame. Then it's divided into two blocks of time.

Nonetheless, be careful. This approach is not effective when the volatility of the supply assumed makes the premiums irrational. Smaller merchants will be forced to purchase at rates off - the-money strike because they have inadequate resources. To order to be close to the current market price, the average monthly range will advise traders to miss option trading or use a debit spread approach.

At any given time, the average monthly amount can be used in any market. It does not need to be used alone, however. An examination of the business trend must also be used. This idea just makes it impossible for buyers to buy cheap options with far-out - of-the-money that offer limited returns.

- **ITM, OTM and ATM Options**

ITM (in-the-money), OTM (out-of-the-money), and ATM (at-the-money) are three acronyms that will be frequently referred to in options trading.

ITM options are options that have an intrinsic value. In other words, if they were to be exercised at that point, they would yield some money. Any call option with a strike price less than the market price of the underlying stock/index is an ITM option. Any put option that has a strike-price greater than the market price of the underlying stock/index is an ITM option. The intrinsic value of an ITM option is the positive difference between its underlying stock's market price and the option's strike price.

Let's put it this way – when a stock's price rises and crosses the strike-price of an associated call option, then that call option becomes ITM. Similarly, when a stock's price falls below the strike price of an associated put option, then that put option becomes ITM.

For example, if Stock 'X' is trading at 500, then any put option of X with a strike price greater than 500 is an ITM option, and any call option of X with a strike price less than 500 is an ITM option.

OTM options are the opposite of ITM options. They do not have any intrinsic value. At the time of expiry, every single OTM option expires worthless. Any call option with its strike-price greater than the market price of its underlying stock/index and any put option with its strike-price less than the market price of its underlying stock/index is OTM options.

For example, if stock 'Y' is trading at 500, then all call options of Y with a strike-price greater than 500 and all put options of Y with a strike-price less than 500 are OTM options.

ATM options are such options for which the strike-prices are currently the same as the underlying's market price. Therefore, an ATM option can easily become an OTM option or an ITM option with any change in the market price of the underlying.

The main thing you should know is that at the time of expiry, only ITM options would have any associated value, while at that time, OTM and ATM options would be worthless.

CHAPTER 6:

The Greeks

When it comes to options trading, the various types of risks that come into play are referred to as one of the Greeks. Each variable is then given a different name, and there are different ways to go about, ensuring that each has as little of an effect on your trades as possible. Trading without first taking the time to clearly understand each of the Greeks and what they mean would be like driving in a foreign country where you were unfamiliar with the basic rules of the road or even the language the signs are written in.

When you look at placing a put or call on a specific underlying stock or building your general options trading strategy, it is important to always consider the rewards and risks from three primary areas. The amount of price change, the amount of volatility change, and the relevant amount of time value the option has left. For holders of calls, this risk can further be identified as either price moving in the wrong direction, a decrease in volatility, or they're not enough useful time left on the option in question. On the contrary, sellers face the risk of prices moving in the wrong direction and an increase in volatility but never when it comes to the time value.

When options are combined or traded, you will then want to determine the Greeks related to new results, often referred to as the net Greeks.

This will allow you to determine the new difference between risk and reward and act appropriately. Understanding the various Greeks and what they mean will also allow you to tailor your strategy based on your own aversion to risk. Consider them as starter guideposts to ensure you are on the right track when it comes to seeking out the right options for you. There are numerous Greeks to consider, and each is outlined in detail below:

- **Delta**

When it comes to individual options, Delta is the amount of risk that currently exists that the price of the underlying stock is going to move. If the strike price of an option is the same as the current price of the underlying stock, then that stock can be said to have a Delta of .5. This can further be interpreted as meaning that if the underlying stock moves 1 point, the price of the option will shift .5 points assuming everything else remains the same. The total range Delta can possibly be anywhere from -1 to 1. Puts can be anywhere from -1 to 0, and calls can be anywhere from 0 to 1.

Delta is likely the first measurement of risk that you will always want to consider when it comes to choosing the options that are right for you. It is especially helpful when you are deciding when to buy a put option as you want it to be far enough from the current price to make a profit but not so far as to be unreasonable. In this instance, it is beneficial to know the expected results of paying less in exchange for knowing the Delta is going to be lower as well. This difference can be seen by simply looking at the strike price and watching how it changes with the put price.

As a rule, the less an option costs, the smaller its Delta is going to be. Delta is often linked to the odds that the option will be worth a profit by the time it expires. For example, if you are looking at an option with a Delta of .52, then you can generally assume, all other things being equal, that the option is slightly more likely than 50 percent to end favorably.

- **Vega**

When a position is taken, the risk of change that comes from the volatility of the underlying stock is referred to as the Vega. The level of volatility that an underlying stock has can change even if the price of the stock in question does not change, and regardless of the amount it changes, it can affect the possibility of profits significantly. Successful strategies can be built around both low volatility and high volatility, as well as neutral volatility in some cases. Long volatility options are those that increase in value as their amount of volatility goes up, and short volatility is when the value increases as volatility decrease. Strategies or trades that utilize long volatility are said to have a positive Vega, and those that use short volatility are said to have a negative Vega. Options that have a neutral level of volatility can be said to have a neutral Vega as well.

As a rule, the more time standing between an option and its expiration date, the higher that option's Vega is going to be. This is because time value is proportional to volatility as the longer the timeline, the greater the chance of volatility eventually happening will be. For example, if a certain $4 option's underlying stock is currently trading around $90 with a Vega of .1 and a volatility of 20 percent. If the volatility increases, just 1 percent would be seen by an increase of 10 cents to a total of $4.10. If the volatility had instead decreased, the price of the $4 option would have decreased by 10 cents instead, leaving a total of $3.90. The amount of change that is seen in an option with a shorter period is often going to result in larger changes because there is ultimately less time the option will restabilize.

- **Theta**

Theta measures the rate at which the time the option has left is disappearing or decaying. This number is frequently going to be negative for your purposes. The moment you purchase an option, your Theta on that option begins decreasing, which means the total value of the option begins to decrease as well because options are considered more valuable the longer the time they insure against new risk. If the amount of Delta on an option exceeds the Theta, then the option is considered profitable for the holder. If Theta instead exceeds the Delta, the profits go to the writer.

For example, if an option has a Thea of 0.015, then it is going to be worth 1.5 cents less tomorrow than it is right now. Puts have negative thetas, and calls have positive thetas. This is because puts are worth the least when they are about to expire, and calls are worth the most because the difference between the starting and ending amounts is going to be at its highest. Additionally, Theta fluctuates day today as it starts off slow and then builds in intensity the closer the option gets to its ultimate expiration. This explains why long-term options attract buyers, and short-term options are preferred by sellers.

If you are planning a trade that has the market remaining neutral, then it is important to take Theta into account, but otherwise, it is less likely to play into your strategy. Regardless, a general rule of thumb is to aim to purchase an option with the lowest Theta rate as possible.

- **Gamma**

If Delta can be thought of as the amount of change that the option will experience when the underlying stock changes, then Gamma can be thought of as the measurement of how the Delta is likely going to change over time. Gamma increases as options near the point where the price of the option and the price of the underlying stock intersect and decreases the further below the strike price the price of the underlying stock drops. Larger Gammas are risky, but they also offer higher returns on average. Gamma is also likely to increase as a specific option nears its ultimate expiration date. This can be taken a step further with the Gamma of the Gamma, which considers the rate the Delta changes at.

For example, if a stock is trading at about $50 and a related option is currently going for $2. If it has a delta of .4 as well as a gamma of .1, then, if the stock increase by $1, the delta will see an increase of 10 percent, which is also the gamma amount. If volatility is low, then gamma is high when the option in question is above its strike price and low when it is below it. Gamma tends to stabilize when volatility is high and decreases when it is low.

▪ Rho

Rho is the name for the risk relating to if the interest rates related to the option in question are going to change before its expiration. When it comes to choosing the system that is right for you, Rho will be unlikely to factor into the equation in most instances. As interest rates increase, call prices will do the same while the price of puts will decrease, and the reverse is true when interest rates decrease. Rho values are typically at their peak when the price of the underlying stock crosses the price of the option in question. Likewise, this value is always going to be negative when it comes to puts and positive when it comes to calls. Rho values are more important when it comes to long options and virtually irrelevant for most short options.

▪ Find the Greeks

When it comes to determining Greeks, it is important to keep in mind that most strategies will have either a negative or a positive value. For example, a positive Vega position will see gains when volatility rises, and a negative Delta position will see a decrease when the underlying stock decreases. Keeping an eye on the Greeks and noting how they change is key to options trading success in both the short and the long term.

When it comes to finding the Greeks for any option, the first thing you will want to keep in mind is that the results you get are always going to be theoretical, no matter how good they end up looking. They are simply projections based on a mathematical formula with various variables plugged in when needed. These include the bid you are putting on the option, the asking price, the last price, the volume, and occasionally the interest.

o **Risk Management**

There will always be risks, and you simply have to learn to manage them and minimize them as much as possible. Your aim should definitely be how you can make huge profits on the trades. There is some risk associated with every investment you make, and options are no different. The risk tolerance threshold of every person is different, and there is nothing wrong with that. You should not force yourself and stretch too thin otherwise; you will be the one left with nothing. Trading should always be done with that money which you can afford to lose. Although options trading has a lot of benefits, they also have great risks, you will learn how you can reduce those risks.

▪ **Diversify Your Portfolio**

Arranging your portfolio should be done with care because it can really help you in minimizing your risks to a great extent. To protect your portfolio, you need to diversify your investments. The idea is very simple. When there are multiple investments in a portfolio, it has lower risk since it poses higher returns, especially when compared to a portfolio containing individual investments only. One way of doing it is to choose the investments that differ in their rate of returns. You can also choose to invest in different sectors and not put all your investments in a single sector.

- **Always Have a Plan**

If you want to take options trading seriously, then it is extremely necessary to have a plan. This plan should have all the steps that you want to take and everything that you want to do. It would be even better if you write it all down. Some beginners go all in, and they literally jump into the trade without knowing much about it. They have this attitude where they want to make as much money as they can, but let me tell you something — this is an absolutely horrible strategy to follow. This is because the plan does not involve any strategy at all, and you do not have any enter or exit plan in the trade. Basically, nothing is in place. If you are of the idea that you are going to wing it with options trading, then trust me, you better give up now; otherwise, you are going to face huge losses.

So, when you make the plan, make sure that you have made it as detailed as possible. The first thing that you have to figure out is your expectation regarding how much profit you want to make through options trading. But this does not mean jotting down whatever figure comes to your mind. You have to be realistic about your expectations. In the first year of options trading, you are not going to make millions, so quit having such high expectations. Another thing that you can do is make a note of all the things that are required when you decide to buy an option, and you should also note down what you want to see in each of those options.

Next, you can make a list of the strategies you want to implement. By now, you must have realized that there are tons of strategies that can be used, but what you will be using will depend on the type of situation you are in. The strategy also depends on the option you have chosen. Remember that you don't need to keep working with one single option throughout.

If you change them in the right situation, then you can even have the chance to make more money, especially if you consider the long term. But do you know why I am asking you to write down the strategies? It is because of a very simple reason, and that is — when you write down the strategies, they automatically become simpler, and you can keep track of them in the same place. It will also help you make more money by choosing the right options.

Another thing to keep in mind is that you always need to have an exit strategy. And you need to figure it out before you even step into a trade. For starters, you need to think as to how much money you are actually willing to lose, or rather you can afford to lose.

You also need to make a note of the conditions during which you will step out of the trade at all costs. Do you know what happens to those who do not have this information in place? They lose a lot of money simply because they do not know when to exit from trade, and they keep going even when it costs them everything. This happens mostly when someone is doing well and so giving up or leaving at the right time becomes quite difficult for them. This also happens when people stay in the trade because they are trying hard to gain back all the money that they have lost, but this only makes them lose more money. So, when you have that exit strategy in place, you know what you have to do when things go south. So, having an exit strategy is truly one of the most important things in risk management.

- **Never Skip on Research**

It is true that with options trading, you can make some handsome amount of money, but it is also true that you need to devote your time and effort and wait patiently before you get handsome results.

Doing your research thoroughly is very important, and you can call it a prerequisite for making a profit in the world of options trading. And if you are a beginner, it means that you have to do a lot of research because you start with nothing. But don't worry, once you start the research, everything will start falling into place. You need to learn different ways of studying the market, and you also need to understand how to figure out the best time to invest in the market. Then, you also have to learn different strategies and know when to use what. But yes, in the beginning, you have to start by learning what options are and what is the difference between options and other forms of investments in the stock market.

There is basically no end to the amount of research you can do. So, take your time and learn it step by step. Don't rush into it and understand everything that you learn. Only then can you stay in the world of options trading in the long-term.

- **Learn to Manage Your Emotions**

Emotions have the tendency to force people into making decisions that will work against them and make them lose money. It can be in any form. Sometimes people stay in the market more than it is necessary and sometimes, people leave too early and both these situations can make you lose money. Also, every successful trader has gone through a phase where they became emotional, but in the end, they learned to control themselves. So, even if you became emotional this one time, there is no need to beat yourself up for it. Learn from your mistakes, and then grow from there. You cannot let your emotions control your decisions; otherwise, making profits will become impossible.

If you have this basic nature of being too stubborn or emotional, then options trading is something that you should not consider right now. In this form of trading, you have to stick to the plan if you want things to work out in your favor. So, if you think you cannot do that and you might become impulsive, then work on dealing with that first before you enter options trading. At times, options trading can get really emotional, causing you to become overwhelmed, panicked, or even too happy from the profits you made. Some people are inherently good at managing their emotions, and it comes naturally to them, but not everyone is like that. So, before you go in and risk all your savings, it is time to ask yourself what kind of person you really are, and are you suitable to dive into options trading right now?

- **Always Keep an Eye on the Features Offered by Your Broker**

Some people think that the broker is only the person who will perform some trades and help you with things you cannot understand, but there is a lot more to it than this. There will be times when you did not make the right call, but your broker might be able to help you out of the situation in some ways. One of how brokers can help you is by providing an out-of-the-money rate. Options trading has a major drawback, that is, at times, people have the possibility of losing their entire money, but when your broker offers you out-of-the-money rates, then you will not go entirely broke and manage to get some of the money back. This is basically an agreement that the investor will make with the broker where the broker agrees to pay a certain amount of money invested back to the investor. Indeed, you will still lose some money, but at least you will not lose it all.

- **Manage Your Money Efficiently**

There will be both good and bad times in trade, and you will have to know how you can manage your money in both these situations. The first thing that you have to learn is to come up with a full-proof plan for managing the money. You also need to understand that losing is something that can happen to anyone, be it a beginner or an expert. It can be a series of losses, or it can also be just one loss. This is mostly because the market is never stagnant, and it keeps changing from time to time, and this is something that no human being can control. But do you know why I am asking you to realize the fact that losses are totally normal? This is because when you do that, you will be building the right mindset for the trade.

Once you understand the fact that losing money is totally normal and can happen to anyone, you will be able to walk on the path of controlling the amount of money that you can possibly lose. This is also where the importance of exit strategy comes in. When you have these plans figured out right from the beginning, you will see for yourself what a big difference it can make to your trading experience. And of course, having planned it all is definitely one of the greatest determinants of success in options trading.

- **Always Monitor Your Trades**

Monitor your chosen option and see how it is performing. This will also ensure that you can make smart decisions. You will know when you need to hold on to it or when you need to sell it so that you can minimize your losses or maximize your profit. All of these things are so important, and the choices you make will directly influence your profit potential. And if you do not keep track of your trades and monitor them, how are you going to know whether they are performing well or not?

Conclusion

Y ou can start trading options by only spending a few hundred dollars. This means you can take small risks and build up your account gradually. Even the best traders experience losses, it is part of the business. But, if you proceed strategically, you will learn how to trade effectively, and you can rack up much more wins than losses.

The best suggestion is to get started with some calls and puts on index funds. Start small, do not force the time, let your account grow, and be comfortable during your constant growth.

If you play your cards right, really study the market and make sound decisions – you will feel confident and proud of your profits.

On the next pages, you will find the most important terminology to be mastered in trading.

Options Trading Terminology

Bid spread: This is the actual difference between the asking price and the bid price for a given option during a particular options trading period.

Big chicken trade: This is a term used to describe a series of bull call calendars, and the bear put calendars.

Break-even point: This is the specific price that an underlying asset must reach to avoid the option buyer from acquiring losses if at all, they decided to exercise the option.

Bullish: This term is particularly referring to an investor who believes that a specific stock price will go higher or simply the market will rise higher.

Call option: This is an equity agreement that awards a buyer the chance to purchase 100 particular shares at a particular strike price within a specified time. A seller is also needed to sell off the stock at a particular price if the option gets exercised.

Credit: It is any value amount received in a particular trading account from the financial benefits experienced in various options trading activities. The profits and multiple benefits feed the trading accounts.

Change: The percentage term price of the last hour's sale in the options market.

Commission: This is the fee charged in an options trading market after option orders have been executed on a securities exchange.

Contract: This is an agreement set between a buyer trader and a seller trader during a particular options trading activity.

Credit: It is any value amount received in a particular trading account from the financial benefits experienced in various options trading activities. The profits and multiple benefits feed the trading accounts.

Debit: This is any amount of cash paid out to purchase an option during a particular trading period.

Dip in the money: This is a term used to refer to multiple in-the-money occurrences that have been experienced in a particular trading period in the options market.

Downside risk: This is the estimation of a particular downfall market price that is likely to be experienced by the market during the end of a particular trading period.

Equity option: It is a kind of option that gives the owner, who happens to be the buyer, the chance to purchase and sell any available stock in the trading market at a specific share during a particular period before the expiration date is reached.

Ex-dividend: This is the actual date in which the stock enters the options trading market with the absence of dividends.

Expiry date: This is the actual date–day, month, or year–to which a particular options trading contract becomes invalid and null.

Front-month: When the expiration of two months is involved in options trading, the month nearer in time is normally considered.

Historical volatility: This is analyzing the actual volatility of the past market occurrences and making the necessary helpful strategies and learning in your trading plan.

Holder: The specific owner of the contract is referred to as the holder in options trading.

Horizontal: This is a term describing the options of the same strike price experienced in different months.

Implied volatility: This is an estimation of the future likelihood market volatility by analyzing the market status through the current activities occurring at the options trading market. Some traders get to use this as one of their strategies the options trading market to acquire large chunks of profits.

Index option: This is an option contract where the index is the underlying stock and not shares of any specific stock.

In the money: All the strike prices possess some intrinsic value where for a call, all strike prices are below the equity price, whereas, for a put, all prices are the ones above the price of the equity.

Last sale: It is the latest price that a certain option trader has traded within options trading.

Long Option: This simply implies having purchased an option at online transactions and therefore own it.

Margin: This is a particular amount of loan offered by a particular broker of a specific trader during a particular trading period.

Mean: This is a mathematical operation where the total sum of observations in the market is divided by the particular number of observations in the market. The mean is used to provide data on various market values and the market standard deviation.

Open interest: This is the number of the option that has been sold and also the ones that have not been brought back or, in any case, exercise.

Option: It is a contract that allows an investor to purchase and sell a specific trading stock at a particular price within a particular period.

Option spread: It is established by buying and selling equal amounts of options of a similar class with the same underlying security. However, the strike prices and expiration dates of the options are different.

Premium: This is the amount of income received by an option trader as he or she writes a contract off to another party.

Put option: The kind of option where a buyer is given the privilege to sell 100 shares at a constant price before the expiration date. On another hand, the seller of a put option is required to purchase stock at a particular price if the trading option gets exercised at all.

Resistance: This is a particular level where the equity price cannot beyond any way higher, meaning that that particular price is the actual price limit.

Selling to open: This ideally describes the selling of a particular option to open a position.

Selling to close: Selling a close means selling a specific option with the desire to close a particular position during options trading.

Short Option: This means to have sold the option in an opening transaction.

Stock: It is described as a portion of a particular company belonging or ownership.

Spread: This is an option position established when a purchase of one option is established and a sale of an option too using the same underlying asset available in the trading market.

Strike price: This is the actual amount of price in which you choose to sell or buy options when you decide to exercise an option in the market.

Time decay: This is the erosion period when the value of time of a specific option diminishes as the expiration date reaches.

Time value: It describes the value to which time is attributable in options before particular expiration date is reached.

Trading platform: This is a general trading site that traders interact with while making trading moves, buying, selling, and any other trading activities. Trading platforms consist of various kinds according to different variety of interests, and a trader gets to pick on a site in which he or she is most comfortable with.

Printed by BoD™in Norderstedt, Germany

9 781803 253923